# BURIED IN PLAIN SIGHT

*When the law becomes the weapon, the truth learns to hide.*

An Elena Ward Legal Thriller — Book One

*John Gates*

**Disclaimer**



This is a work of fiction. Names, characters, businesses, organisations, places, events, and incidents are either the product of the author's imagination or used fictitiously. Any resemblance to actual persons, living or dead, or actual events is purely coincidental.

This novel depicts legal procedures, law enforcement practices, and courtroom dynamics for dramatic and narrative purposes. These portrayals are fictional and do not represent actual legal standards, processes, or advice. The author has taken creative liberties throughout.

*'The most dangerous lies are the ones written in legal language. They survive because we are trained to trust the form.'*

*— Daniel Ward, personal journal, March 2019*

## Chapter One
## The Routine Review

The rain had returned just after sunset, tapping gently against the tall windows of Lang & Associates' document review room. It was the kind of rain Brisbane saved for the end of long days — patient, relentless, indifferent to the people still inside.

The skyline shimmered beyond the glass, blurred by moisture and the haze of late summer humidity. Streetlights cast golden halos into the mist below. The river wound through the city like a dark ribbon, carrying the scent of damp earth and eucalyptus through the building's ventilation — a reminder that the lush world beyond her isolated workspace had not stopped moving simply because she had.

Inside, Elena Ward sat alone.

She was surrounded by towers of legal binders and the soft, neutral hum of fluorescent lights. The document review room occupied the far corner of the firm's fourteenth floor, rarely used except for deep archival work. It smelled of paper, aged coffee, and the particular silence of a place where no one came unless they had to. To Elena, that silence was a luxury. It gave her space to think, to breathe, to dig.

At twenty-nine, she was a junior associate with a reputation for precision that occasionally unnerved her seniors. She had joined Lang & Associates two years ago, fresh from graduating at the top of her cohort at UQ Law. Her peers had dispersed to the city's corporate towers — the prestige firms, the glass and marble. Elena had chosen differently. A mid-sized practice meant real clients, real consequences, real weight.

Her appearance was professional but deliberate: a navy blazer over a cream blouse, her mahogany hair pulled into a tight bun. Her hazel eyes — sharp, observant, often described by colleagues as unreadable — scanned each contract page with practiced efficiency. Her mixed heritage, Anglo-Australian and Filipino, meant she had spent her life occupying the margins of other people's categories. She had stopped trying to fit them.

Tonight she was reviewing documents for Morrison v. Fortis Constructions, a minor residential dispute that had been passed to her because no one else wanted it. Too old. Too small. Too routine, they said.

Elena did not believe in routine.

She worked through the contract methodically — Termination, Indemnity, Liability — until page thirty-one stopped her cold.

Clause 14.7. Deferred Risk Allocation.

The language was unusual. Evasive in a way that standard construction contracts never were. It referenced 'temporary structural exemptions' and 'non-binding safety waivers' — terms with no precedent in the firm's template library. The clause had clearly been inserted manually. It read less like a standard provision and more like something designed to be overlooked.

Elena reread it twice. Then a third time.

She opened the firm's digital archive and ran a search. Three results came back — all Fortis Constructions projects, all containing a version of Clause 14.7, all in buildings that had reported structural issues within five years of completion.

Her pulse quickened.

She glanced at the photograph tucked into the corner of her notebook: her brother Daniel, grinning in a hard hat, standing beside a half-built tower. He had died in a scaffolding collapse on a Fortis Constructions site. The case had been quietly settled. No charges. No accountability.

Elena had stopped believing in accidents around the same time she stopped believing in routine.

She saved the contracts to a secure folder on her laptop and backed everything up to an encrypted drive. Then she reached for her phone to photograph the clause — and paused.

The room was too quiet.

She glanced at the door. It was closed. Had it been open earlier? She shook it off. Fatigue. The particular paranoia of late nights in a room where every sound had room to echo.

Her phone buzzed.

A message from Liz Tran, the firm's newest paralegal: Sorry to intrude so late, but I found something odd in the Morrison case files. Can I drop by?

Liz appeared minutes later — rain-soaked umbrella in one hand, battered folder in the other. She was petite, sharp-eyed, with dark curls escaping a loose ponytail and an energy that seemed to crackle even in the after-hours hush. She had been with the firm only a month, but she noticed things others missed. Elena had already learned to trust that instinct.

'I hope I'm not interrupting,' Liz said, setting the folder on the table between them.

'Not at all. What did you find?'

'A discrepancy in the Ashbourne project timelines. Some invoices don't match the official construction schedule.' She paused, fingers hovering over the tabs. 'I thought it might be nothing. But given who's involved...'

The sentence trailed off deliberately. Liz Tran did not finish sentences carelessly.

For the first time since Daniel's death, Elena felt something she hadn't expected: the faint, cautious warmth of not being alone in a room that mattered.

She would need it.

• • •

The following morning, Elena knocked on Victor Lang's office door with the contract under her arm and the clause marked in red. Victor was the firm's founding partner — charismatic, respected, known for his ability to make complicated things seem simple. His office occupied a corner of the fourteenth floor with floor-to-ceiling windows on two sides and a wall of law books behind him that had not been touched since the year they were shelved.

He looked up from his desk. 'Come in.'

She placed the contract in front of him. 'Clause 14.7.'

He examined it, eyebrow raised. 'You're reviewing documents for a minor property dispute.'

'Three other Fortis Constructions projects contain a version of this clause. All three buildings reported structural failures.'

Victor leaned back, steepled his fingers. 'Elena. You're building a conspiracy theory from a contract clause.'

'I'm identifying a pattern.'

He studied her. Something shifted in his expression — not quite discomfort, but close. 'My brother died on one of their sites,' she said quietly.

The discomfort deepened. He let a beat pass before he spoke. 'Grief can make patterns out of coincidence. Be careful.'

'I'm not grieving,' she said. 'I'm reading.'

She walked back to the review room. When she arrived, her files were gone.

The binders. The printouts. The notes. Only her laptop remained — disconnected from the firm's network. She checked the system logs. Her access had been flagged. Restricted.

That evening, back in her apartment, her phone buzzed with a message from an unknown number.

*'You're not the only one digging. Someone inside Fortis is watching. Be careful.'*

Elena stared at the screen for a long time.

The clause wasn't forgotten at all. It was protected. And someone very much did not want it found.

## Chapter Two
## What Routine Hides

Sleep was fitful. Elena woke before dawn, her mind already running — fragments of the anonymous message looping behind her eyes, the chill of her apartment pressing in from every direction. She had left the bedroom window cracked. Brisbane in summer meant the choice between heat and vulnerability, and lately she had been choosing heat.

She sat at her kitchen table in the dark, both hands around a chipped mug of tea, watching the city gradually lighten through the glass. Her laptop sat open on the table, but its screen had gone to sleep. She had not typed a word in an hour.

You're not the only one digging. Someone inside Fortis is watching.

She replayed the past week methodically, the way she had been trained to: not looking for what was wrong, but for what didn't belong. The flagged login. The particular stillness in the office kitchen when she had mentioned Fortis Constructions' name — a conversation that should have drawn polite indifference but had instead produced a silence that was too considered, too swift. The spreadsheet she had begun assembling at home in the evenings, incident reports cross-referenced against inspection schedules, safety certifications mapped against project timelines. The gaps in that spreadsheet. The places where records should exist and didn't.

None of it was proof. Not yet. Not in the way a regulator or a court would require. But Elena had been reading contracts long enough to understand that the absence of a document was itself a document.

A garbage truck made its rounds on the street below. A traffic light cycled patiently for an audience of no one. She watched the sky move from black to the particular grey-blue of a Brisbane morning that hasn't decided yet whether it will be humid or merely warm.

She thought about Daniel.

He would have argued with her about this — that was the thing she missed most. Not the conclusion of an argument but the argument itself, the way he had of pressing on the soft parts of an idea until you had either strengthened them or admitted they weren't there. He had been eight years older than her and had treated her, from the time she could hold a proper conversation, as his intellectual equal. That gift was irreplaceable. She had not found anyone else who argued the same way.

'Be careful, El,' he had said once, not long before he died. They had been at a kitchen table much like this one, over the remains of a late dinner, talking the way they always talked — directly, without the hedging that families sometimes confuse for kindness. 'The truth is often buried beneath layers of legality. It doesn't mean it isn't there. It just means you have to be prepared for what happens when you find it.'

She had teased him about sounding like a first-year philosophy student. He had laughed. Three weeks later he was dead.

Elena stood, rinsed her mug, and made a decision.

She opened her laptop and worked quickly — downloading encrypted backups of every file she had managed to copy before her access was restricted, deleting sensitive material from her phone, creating secure copies in three separate locations she controlled independently of the firm's network. She worked with the focused efficiency of someone who had accepted that the situation was dangerous and decided to proceed anyway, because the alternative was unacceptable.

Daniel had died because someone had decided that profit outweighed safety, and that a contractual clause could carry the weight of that decision invisibly. He had found the clause. He had tried to do something about it. And the system had not protected him.

She was not going to let the same system decide she hadn't looked hard enough.

From her battered leather satchel she retrieved the documents she had taken home: copies of the three archived Fortis Constructions contracts, a coroner's report she had requested through a professional contact, and Daniel's union membership card — old, laminated, worn at the corners. She tucked the card inside the front cover of her notebook. She had carried it for two years. It still felt like weight she needed.

By the time the sun edged above the horizon, Elena had resolved to keep going, however imperfect her evidence, however vague the threats. Her neighbours' kitchen lights blinked on across the courtyard. The city was waking, ordinary and indifferent, going about its ordinary business. Elena shouldered her satchel, locked her apartment, and stepped into the morning.

She was not alone in this fight, she reminded herself. Somewhere, someone else was already watching.

She just needed to find them before the other side did.

## Chapter Three
## **Shadows of Accountability**

*9:00 AM — a café near Lang & Associates*

The morning sun cut through the café windows at a low angle, warm enough to make the room feel earlier than it was. Victor Lang was already seated at a table near the glass when Elena arrived, a flat white in front of him, his silver hair catching the light. He looked older than she remembered from yesterday. Or perhaps she was simply looking more carefully.

'Good morning,' he said, and gestured to the chair across from him. His voice carried the particular warmth of a man who had spent thirty years making clients feel at ease — a warmth Elena had learned to measure rather than trust.

She sat. 'Thanks for meeting me.'

He slid a manila folder across the table. 'I want you to understand that by showing you this, I am asking you to be careful. Not to stop.' A deliberate pause. 'Those are different things.'

Elena opened the folder. Internal emails from Lang's own correspondence logs: management-to-management exchanges about safety audit schedules on two Fortis Constructions projects. The dates told a story. Concerns raised, responses delayed, concerns quietly dropped. Nobody had done anything explicitly wrong — nothing had been formally approved that shouldn't have been — but the rhythm of the correspondence was the rhythm of an organisation that had learned to look away efficiently.

'These don't prove anything on their own,' Elena said.

'No. They establish context.' Victor glanced around the café with the careful casualness of a man checking for something he hopes isn't there. 'Pay attention to the timestamps. People knew. And people decided that knowing was sufficient — that they didn't need to act.' He lowered his voice. 'Fortis is powerful, Elena. If we move against them, we need to move correctly.'

She nodded. 'I understand the risks.'

'I'm not sure you do,' he said, not unkindly. 'Not entirely.'

Their conversation was interrupted by the arrival of Ben Ashford, who approached their table with the slightly self-conscious energy of someone who has unexpectedly encountered two people deep in a serious discussion. Elena had known Ben since law school — bright, affable, more troubled by the corporate world than he generally admitted.

'Elena. Victor.' He pulled up a chair without being invited, because Ben had always done this. 'What's the case?'

Elena looked at Victor. He gave a microscopic shrug.

'We're looking at irregularities in contracts tied to Fortis Constructions,' she said carefully. 'Clause 14.7. It appears across multiple projects. All of them have reported safety failures.'

Ben's expression sharpened. The affability dropped. 'I have a contact inside Fortis. Safety compliance. He's been uneasy for a while — things he's seen that didn't sit right. I never pushed because I didn't know if there was something to push toward.' He looked at her steadily. 'It sounds like there might be now.'

'It would be a risk for him,' Elena said.

'It would.' Ben was quiet for a moment. 'I'll ask him anyway. That's his choice to make, not ours.'

Victor studied his coffee. 'Be discreet.'

'I know how to be discreet,' Ben said, with the mildly offended dignity of a man who considers discretion one of his better qualities.

After Ben left, Victor looked at Elena across the table for a long moment. 'I told you to be careful. I meant it.' He paused. 'I also mean this: don't stop. Just — understand what you're walking toward.'

It was the most honest thing he had said to her in two years.

• • •

*That evening — South Bank Parklands*

She had received the message that afternoon from an unknown number: Meet me at South Bank. 8 PM. I knew your brother.

She had texted back: Who is this?

The reply: You'll understand when you get here.

Against every practical instinct, she went.

South Bank in the evening was bright with families and the smell of food from the riverside stalls. Children ran ahead of their parents along the water's edge. A busker somewhere upstream played something slow and recognisable. The ordinary weight of a Tuesday evening in the city — which made the woman standing alone near the parkland's northern tree line feel all the more out of place.

She was in her late thirties, Elena estimated. Dark coat despite the heat. Dark eyes that had been watching for several minutes before Elena reached her.

'Elena Ward?'

'Yes.'

'I'm Leah Pham. Daniel and I worked on a site together in 2017 — different project, different company, same industry.' Her voice was careful in the way of someone who had rehearsed their opening and was now navigating the gap between preparation and reality. 'When I heard he died, something changed for me. I started paying attention differently. And when I heard you were asking questions about Fortis —'

'How did you hear that?'

'The legal world is smaller than lawyers like to believe.' Leah glanced around once — quickly, professionally — and produced a folder from inside her coat. 'I've been collecting these for three years. Management correspondence showing they were aware of structural problems and chose to manage the paperwork rather than the problems. Names. Dates. Internal risk assessments that never left the building.'

Elena took the folder. In the pale light from the riverbank she could see enough to understand its weight.

'This could expose them,' she said quietly.

‘It could,’ Leah said. ‘If it’s handled correctly.’ She left the alternative unspoken, which was more eloquent than any ending would have been. ‘I need you to understand what happens to people who get in front of this thing and stumble.’

‘I understand.’

Leah studied her for a moment with the attention of someone deciding whether to believe what they’re being told. Then she nodded — once, slowly. ‘Then we need somewhere safer than a park bench.’

They found a quiet corner table at a café on Grey Street, away from the windows. Elena spent the next hour going through the folder while Leah talked — quietly and precisely — about what she had seen and what she believed it meant.

By the time they left, something had been established between them that Elena did not yet have a name for. It was more than an alliance. It was the beginning of a shared accountability.

She was nearly at her car when the message arrived.

Victor: Be careful. I’ve heard whispers that Fortis might be looking into you.

She looked at it for a moment, then put her phone away and drove home through the dark, the folder on the passenger seat beside her, Daniel’s voice somewhere at the edge of her thoughts.

‘Be careful, El. The truth is often buried beneath layers of legality.’

She was beginning to understand what he had meant.

## Chapter Four
**Beneath the Surface**

The morning heat came early. Elena arrived at the old Riverside site before seven — a decommissioned construction zone on the south bank, cordoned off behind cyclone fencing, its half-finished skeleton of concrete and rebar standing against the pale sky like something interrupted mid-sentence.

Leah was already there, pacing a slow line along the fence, her expression set in the particular way of someone who has been alert for a long time and is managing the fatigue of it.

'I've been hearing things,' Leah said without preamble. 'Fortis has tightened internal security. People inside are being watched. Someone mentioned my name in a context I don't fully understand yet, and that's never comfortable.'

Elena felt the familiar cold settling at the base of her spine. 'How serious?'

'Serious enough that I'm standing at a fence at seven in the morning instead of somewhere I could have coffee.'

They moved along the perimeter without entering. Leah produced a second folder from her bag: photographs of construction sites taken at angles that suggested someone who knew how to document conditions without making it obvious. Inspection reports marked as completed on dates when the site had clearly not been inspected. A roster of subcontractors that did not match the workers actually present on several Fortis projects.

Elena photographed each document methodically, saying nothing until she had finished.

‘The names of workers willing to testify,’ Leah said, pointing to the last page. ‘Three of them. All scared. All certain. I’ve told them nothing about you — if they’re going to come forward, that needs to be their own decision.’

‘I understand.’ Elena lowered the phone. ‘Are you safe?’

Leah considered this with genuine seriousness rather than reflexive reassurance. ‘Probably. For now.’ A pause. ‘Check in with me tomorrow.’

They heard footsteps — a group of men in hard hats rounding the far corner of the building. One of them glanced toward the fence line. Elena and Leah stepped back behind a concrete support pillar without discussing it.

The men moved past.

‘We need to be finished here,’ Leah said quietly.

They separated at the car park. Elena reached her car and sat for a moment with the engine off. Her phone buzzed: Ben Ashford.

My contact is willing to meet. But he wants to know who else is involved before he commits to anything.

She typed back: Tell him discretion is absolute on our side. No names until he’s comfortable.

She was about to start the engine when she noticed it — a dark sedan parked across the car park, engine idling, a figure in the driver’s seat who was not looking at his phone or the road or anything in particular. He was looking at her car.

Elena kept her expression neutral. Started her engine. Drove out at an ordinary speed, turned right rather than left, away from her usual route home.

She spent twelve minutes on a series of turns she had no practical reason to make, watching the mirror. The sedan did not follow. Either she was mistaken, or they were better at this than a sedan in a car park suggested. Neither option was particularly reassuring.

That night at her kitchen table, the documents spread around her laptop, she drafted a preliminary memo: the clause, its variants, the pattern of structural failures, the timeline of Victor's correspondence, the worker testimonies she had not yet obtained but believed she could get. She wrote it with precision — every claim sourced, every inference clearly labelled as an inference.

She did not send it. She saved it to the encrypted drive, then sat for a while in the quiet of the apartment.

The truth was buried beneath layers of legality. She was beginning to understand how many layers there were.

## Chapter Five
# The Coordinates

*Friday, 29 March*

The message had arrived on the encrypted channel three days earlier — terse, specific: coordinates, a time, an instruction to come alone, and a name she had not expected to encounter outside of documents. Gareth Lin. Former compliance auditor, Fortis Constructions, 2015 to 2019.

Elena drove north on the Bruce Highway in the late afternoon as the Sunshine Coast range darkened against the sky. The Glass House Mountains appeared in the distance — those ancient volcanic columns her mother had once told her looked like ancestors standing watch. She had been eight years old and had believed it completely. Driving toward them now with a USB drive in her jacket pocket and a voice recorder on the seat beside her, she found the image less comforting than it once had been.

The coordinates resolved to a fire lookout deep in the national park — a place she hadn't visited since a school camp at thirteen. She parked at a rusted gate and walked the last stretch on gravel, through eucalyptus and stringybark, the smell of damp earth and resin thickening as the last of the direct sun dropped behind the ridge.

The lookout was in a state of considered disrepair: half-collapsed, its steel frame rusted to a dark amber, vines threading through the stairs with the patient confidence of something that intends to remain. Elena climbed slowly, testing each step before trusting it.

He was at the top.

Gareth Lin stood with his back to the stairs, looking out over the valley as the last light went out of the sky. He turned at her approach: mid-fifties, a faded windbreaker, eyes that were sharp in the specific way of someone who has spent years watching for danger and learned not to stop.

'You came,' he said.

'You said you knew Daniel.'

'I did.' He poured tea from a thermos into a chipped enamel cup and offered it without ceremony. She took it. The warmth was grounding in a way she hadn't expected to need.

He talked for a long time. The valley below them went from green to grey to black as he spoke.

He had worked for Fortis as a compliance auditor. His job, officially, was to verify that safety inspection records were accurate and complete. His job in practice was to ensure that the records were presentable — which was a different thing entirely. He had been hired during a difficult period: a separation, money problems, a willingness to be practical about what he could afford to know. He had justified it the way people justify things that allow them to continue. He had told himself he was protecting jobs. He had told himself that the gap between records and reality was manageable, that no one would be hurt by a delay that was, after all, only procedural.

He had been telling himself these things when Daniel Ward walked into his office with a USB drive and an expression of calm, clear fury.

'He had procurement records,' Gareth said. 'Inspection logs. All falsified. He'd cross-referenced them against actual site conditions – collecting it for months. He wanted to go public. I told him to wait. Said we needed more.' The pause was long and honest. 'Two weeks later he was dead.'

Elena heard the words land at a slight remove; the way very large things sometimes arrived.

'The scaffolding collapse,' she said.

Gareth shook his head. 'That's what the report says. But I saw the preliminary autopsy – before it was amended. He had defensive injuries. Bruising consistent with a struggle, not a fall. He didn't die in the collapse.' A pause. 'He died after it.'

The valley was completely dark now. Elena kept her hands steady around the cup.

'Why didn't you report what you'd seen?'

'I tried. My apartment was broken into within a week. Laptop taken. Documents gone.' He reached into his bag. 'I had made backups. Hidden them in three locations I'd told nobody about. I've been living with them ever since, trying to decide what to do with information I was too frightened to use and too guilty to destroy.'

He handed her a USB drive. Smaller than the one Daniel had carried to his office. Heavier, somehow, in her palm.

'That's everything. Procurement records. Internal emails. Offshore payment accounts. Bribery payments to three different inspectors.'

He met her eyes. 'And something else. It's not just Fortis. There's a folder on the drive. Open it and you'll understand.'

She drove back in complete silence, the USB in her inside pocket, the Glass House Mountains receding in the mirror. By the time she reached her apartment the rain had started again.

She plugged in the drive. The password prompt appeared. On the slip of paper Gareth had given her, a single instruction: The name of the café where Daniel first told me the truth.

She thought for only a moment. Then she typed: Central Station Café.

The folder opened.

Near the top: Lang Internal. Inside it, a memo. Senior partner to Fortis's legal team. Subject line: Clause 14.7 implementation strategy. The language was precise, professional, and unambiguous about intent. The signature at the bottom belonged to someone she had been introduced to on her first day at the firm.

Elena sat back. The rain tapped steadily against the window.

Her phone buzzed. An unknown number.

'You weren't alone. Someone followed you to the lookout.'

She checked the burner phone Gareth had told her to bring. The device had been cloned. And the second USB drive — the one she had carried into the mountains — had already been accessed remotely.

The leak had begun.

## Chapter Six
## The Leak

Elena sat at her kitchen table and read the message again.

'You weren't alone. Someone followed you to the lookout.'

She set the burner phone face-down on the table with the careful deliberateness of someone managing a reaction they cannot afford to have. Then she picked it up and called Gareth's number.

It rang three times. 'Elena.'

'They cloned the burner. The second drive was accessed remotely. Whatever was on it –'

'I know.' His voice was steady in the way of someone who has been expecting bad news and is therefore less destroyed by its arrival. 'I told you to come alone.'

'I did come alone. Someone was already there.' She kept her voice level. 'They were watching the coordinates, not following me.'

A short silence. 'Then it started before you arrived.' Another pause. 'They're going to move quickly now. We need to be faster.'

Liz arrived forty minutes later, soaked from the rain, a laptop under one arm and a folder marked Tran – Legal Strategy under the other. She was carrying the particular energy of someone who has been thinking hard for several hours and has arrived at conclusions she needs to share immediately.

'Tell me everything,' she said, sitting down across from Elena without removing her wet coat.

Elena told her. All of it: Gareth, the lookout, the memo, the name on the memo, the cloned phone, the accessed drive.

Liz listened without interrupting. When Elena finished, there was a silence of perhaps ten seconds — which, for Liz, was a long time.

'We can't go to the press yet,' she said.

'We have the memo. We have —'

'We have documents that were obtained from a source who will be described as an unstable former employee with a grudge,' Liz said. 'Without forensic verification, without chain of custody, without a protective structure around Gareth and Marcus and you — they will discredit everything inside twenty-four hours and we will have burned our only chance.' She opened her laptop. 'We build the firewall first. Legal, then media, then public. In that order.'

Elena looked at her. 'You've been thinking about this.'

'Since the day I found the invoice discrepancy,' Liz said. 'I just needed to know how deep it went before I could tell you what we were building.'

They worked through the night. Liz drafted a legal strategy framework and reached out to Rafiq Mehta — a digital forensics expert she had worked with previously, whose professional reputation was, according to Liz, impeccable and frankly somewhat intimidating. Elena worked through the documents on the third USB drive, Gareth's personal archive, cross-referencing offshore accounts against public corporate records for the Fortis entities she had already identified.

An hour before dawn, Liz looked up. 'The cloned device means they know we have the drives. They'll send a legal shot across the bow soon — cease and desist, stolen property allegation. Something to rattle us.'

'Let them,' Elena said.

Her phone buzzed. Not the burner — her personal phone. An unknown number, the message written with the clipped precision of a corporate legal team woken at an inconvenient hour: You are in possession of confidential documents belonging to Fortis Constructions Pty Ltd. Return them within 24 hours or face legal action.

Elena showed it to Liz.

'Predictable,' Liz said. She was already typing.

• • •

Three days later they met Gareth at a library in Ipswich — neutral territory, public enough for safety, quiet enough for the conversation they needed to have. He arrived in a hoodie and sunglasses that drew more attention than he probably intended, and he looked thinner than he had at the lookout. The weight of the decision he had made was sitting on him differently in the flat interior light.

'I want to go public,' he said. 'By myself if I have to.'

'Not alone,' Liz said. 'You'd be destroyed before the first article ran.'

'Then together.' He set a third USB drive on the table. 'This is my personal record. Every contract I signed, every meeting I attended, every email I received and sent. My mistakes included.' He looked at Elena. 'I'm not asking to be made innocent. I'm asking to be useful.'

Liz picked up the drive. 'I'll get Rafiq to verify the metadata on all three drives. Once we have forensic authentication, we file a protective injunction and release the first wave simultaneously. Legal journal, investigative outlet, mainstream press. Coordinated. Embargoed until the moment it drops.'

Gareth nodded once. 'And the memo? The one with the partner's name?'

Elena and Liz exchanged a glance. 'That one we handle separately,' Elena said.

That evening, back at Liz's apartment, a message arrived from a blocked number on Liz's secured work line. A name. C. Merrick. An internal ethics memo dated 2017. A reference to Clause 14.7 that should not have existed in the correspondence of someone who was now sitting on the Queensland Supreme Court bench.

The judge assigned to their case.

Liz read it twice. Then she said, carefully: 'This doesn't change the strategy. It accelerates it.'

Elena nodded. Outside the apartment, the rain was picking up — the same patient Brisbane rain that had been present at every stage of this thing, as though it had decided to bear witness.

Her phone buzzed one final time.

'You're not the only one building a case.'

The war for the truth had begun. And they were no longer the only combatants.

Chapter Seven

## The Firewall

They had not slept properly in four days.

Liz's apartment had been converted into something that resembled a very low-budget operations centre: the coffee table buried under printed timelines, the kitchen bench occupied by two laptops and Rafiq Mehta's portable forensic workstation, the whiteboard on the wall carrying a network diagram Liz had drawn and redrawn three times until she was satisfied with its accuracy.

Rafiq had arrived on the second day. He was quiet in the particular way of people who say less because they think more — compact, methodical, with the patience of someone who had spent a significant portion of his professional life waiting for computers to finish tasks that required human attention afterward. He had examined all three USB drives with the thorough care of a surgeon preparing an unfamiliar patient, and his conclusions, delivered without drama, had changed the shape of everything.

'The files are authentic,' he told them, without looking up from his screen. 'Metadata consistent. No signs of tampering or fabrication. Chain of custody can be established from the source files on the drives to the copies here.' He paused. 'There's something else. On the second drive — the one that was accessed remotely — I can see exactly what they retrieved. They got the financial records and the offshore accounts. They did not get the memo.'

'Why not?' Elena asked.

'It was in a subdirectory that wasn't indexed correctly. A filing error from whoever organised the original archive.' He looked up. 'Gareth's disorganisation saved us.'

Liz was already on the phone to a lawyer in Sydney, arguing — with the measured force of someone who knows she is right and is willing to wait until the other party understands this — for the terms of a protective injunction that would cover Gareth, Marcus, and Elena herself. Elena listened to one side of the conversation and took notes.

Marcus Hall had made contact two days ago. A short, encrypted message through a channel he should not have had access to: I need to speak with you. Not at the firm. The initial M.

They had met at a café near Roma Street Station. Marcus was in his early fifties, silver-haired, carrying a gravitas he had spent his career trying to moderate. He sat across from Elena and came directly to the point.

'I've seen the memo. The Lang Internal document. I know what it means, and I know that you know what it means.'

Elena said nothing. Let him continue.

'I raised concerns about Clause 14.7 in 2018. Through the ethics committee. In writing.' His jaw tightened slightly. 'I was told to stay in my lane. The memo from that meeting was not preserved in the usual records.' He looked at her steadily. 'I preserved my own copy.'

She sat forward. 'Will you testify?'

'If you can protect my family during and after the proceedings, yes.' He paused. 'I have children. I need that to be explicit, not implied.'

'I'll make it explicit,' Elena said.

Back at the apartment, she relayed the conversation to Liz and Rafiq. The effect on Liz was immediate and visible: her whole posture shifted, the way a ship shifts when a counterweight is properly placed.

'An internal ethics complaint, contemporaneously documented, that was suppressed,' Liz said. 'That's not just corroboration. That's foundation.'

She opened the media cascade spreadsheet — columns of names, outlets, embargo dates, release packages — and added Marcus's name to the witness column.

'Thursday morning,' she said. 'We go live Thursday. Simultaneous drop. The Brief gets the legal analysis of Clause 14.7 and the whistleblower protections framework. The Signal gets the investigative piece — everything from the clause to the offshore accounts. ABC News gets the public summary, with Gareth's testimony and Marcus's confirmation of the internal suppression.'

'And the memo?' Elena asked.

'Not yet. We name Lang in the filings, but we don't release the memo publicly until after the injunction is granted. We need it in the court record first — protected — or they'll challenge its provenance before anyone has a chance to understand what it says.'

Elena nodded. It was the right call.

The following morning, a cease-and-desist arrived from Fortis's legal team. An hour later, a formal complaint was filed with the

Queensland Law Society against Elena personally. An hour after that, Rafiq called from the kitchen.

'They're probing the cloud vault. Someone is attempting to spoof your credentials.'

'Can they get in?'

'No. But they're trying, which means they know the vault exists.' He paused. 'I've added another layer. We should assume they'll escalate.'

That afternoon her phone displayed a message from an unknown number: You're being watched. Marcus is compromised.

She showed it to Liz.

'Divide and fracture,' Liz said, without hesitation. 'Classic. They want you second-guessing the people you need most. We hold the line. We don't change the strategy, and we don't change the Thursday timeline.'

Elena held.

Late that evening, as Rafiq shut down his workstation and Liz fell asleep on the couch surrounded by legal briefs, Elena stood at the kitchen window and looked out at the city. The lights on the river. The ordinary movement of people going about a world that did not yet know what was about to be released into it.

Thursday was three days away.

She thought about Daniel, as she often did in quiet moments — not with grief anymore, exactly, but with the particular clarity of someone who has finally found a use for what they have been carrying.

Hold the line. She could hold the line.

## Chapter Eight
# The Insider

*Thursday, 6:00 AM*

Liz was already awake when Elena emerged from the spare bedroom, already dressed, already at her laptop with a coffee that looked as though it might be her second.

'Good morning,' Elena said.

'It will be,' Liz replied, and hit send.

The packages went simultaneously to three separate email addresses. The legal brief to The Brief. The investigative file to The Signal. The public summary to ABC News. Each release timed to land at once, each package encrypted and watermarked with unique metadata trails so that any subsequent leak could be traced to its source.

Liz leaned back. 'Now we wait approximately two hours for the world to catch up.'

She was off by thirty minutes.

By eight o'clock the story was trending. By nine, Lang & Associates had issued a statement — Lang & Associates categorically denies any wrongdoing and is conducting a thorough internal review — which Liz read aloud in the tone of someone reading a prediction they wrote themselves and are now mildly gratified to find accurate.

Elena's inbox transformed over the following hour from a professional tool into something closer to a live feed: messages of support, legal threats, interview requests, and messages from journalists she had never heard of. And one message, from a blocked number, that said simply: I saw the drop. You did it.

She typed back: Gareth?

The reply came immediately: Safe. For now. But I have something else. Something I didn't give you.

They met that afternoon at a nondescript motel near Caboolture, off the highway, the kind of place that takes cash and hasn't updated its signage since 2003. Gareth arrived looking hollowed out — lighter in the face, steadier in the eyes, as though making the decision to go public had removed a weight even as it had added others.

He handed her a small audio recorder. Old. The kind with physical buttons.

'Daniel,' he said. 'The night before he died.'

Elena looked at the recorder for a moment. Then she pressed play.

The voice was Daniel's. Clear, calm, with the particular quality of someone speaking for the record rather than for an audience — choosing words carefully because he believed they might need to stand alone later.

'If anything happens to me, it's not an accident. I've named names. I've filed reports. I've done everything I was supposed to do, and I've documented all of it. If they bury me, someone needs to dig me out.'

A long silence on the recording. Then, quieter: 'Elena — if you're hearing this — don't be careful. Be right.'

She pressed stop. Outside, the highway ran its ordinary traffic past the window. She sat with the recorder in her hands for a long time.

Gareth spoke quietly. 'He believed you would come. He told me your name. He said if anything happened, eventually you would find your way to this.'

Liz, who had come with Elena and was sitting on the edge of the room's other chair, spoke first. 'We release this. Carefully. Sequenced after the legal filings, before the public phase.' Her voice was firm but not hard. 'It's more powerful than any document we have, which means we have to protect it from being called manipulative. The framing has to be precise.'

'Agreed,' Elena said.

She looked at Gareth. 'Are you ready for what comes after Thursday?'

He thought about it honestly — actually thought, rather than reaching for reassurance. 'No,' he said finally. 'But I'm done hiding. Those aren't the same thing.'

• • •

Back in Brisbane, Marcus Hall gave his sealed deposition that afternoon, guided by Rafiq's secure platform, his testimony recorded with forensic care. He was precise, specific, and wept exactly once — briefly, when recounting the moment he had understood that his suppressed ethics complaint had preceded Daniel Ward's death by eleven months.

When the deposition concluded he said, more to himself than to the room: 'I stayed silent too long.'

Nobody argued.

That evening, Lang & Associates filed a defamation suit. Fortis Constructions retained additional senior counsel. And somewhere in the firm's internal records, according to a message Rafiq received from a contact at a federal oversight agency, a document was being systematically scrubbed by someone with admin-level access who knew exactly what they were looking for.

The same access level as a senior partner.

'They're scared,' Liz said.

'Good,' Elena said. 'They should be.'

Chapter Nine

## The Pressure Point

She left her phone behind. The instructions had been specific — no phones, no press, no Liz — and while Elena had spent an hour arguing internally about the wisdom of compliance, she concluded that refusing the conditions of a meeting with Malcolm Venn was less interesting than having it.

The Kangaroo Point Cliffs at dusk were populated with the particular mixture of people who gather at the edges of things: runners, photographers, couples standing at the railing looking out at the river and the city beyond it. The lights were beginning to come on across the Brisbane skyline, office towers illuminating floor by floor, the city performing its ordinary drama against the fading sky.

Venn found her before she found him.

He had the quality, Elena had observed from across conference tables, of a man who always arrived slightly before the moment required. Sixty-two, she estimated. Lean in the way of someone who has always been careful about how he appeared. He wore a dark jacket despite the heat and carried himself with the composed authority of a senior partner so accustomed to being the most powerful person in a room that he had never quite learned to be anything else.

'You've been busy,' he said, falling into step beside her along the cliff path.

'I read the memo,' she replied.

He was quiet for a moment. The city moved below them. 'I designed the clause,' he said. 'Not alone, and not without instruction, but it originated with me. The concept, the language, the strategy for deploying it across multiple projects with sufficient variation that the pattern wouldn't be obvious.' A pause. 'I was very good at my job.'

She kept walking. Said nothing.

'What you don't know yet,' Venn continued, 'is the size of what surrounds it. Fortis isn't the client at the centre of this — they're significant, but they're not the architecture. There are government contacts, state and federal. Auditing firms whose principals have been receiving payments through the same offshore structures. Two other law firms who were given versions of the clause and told it was standard industry practice.' He looked at her sideways. 'If this goes to trial, it doesn't just burn Lang. It burns a system.'

'I know,' Elena said.

'Do you want that?'

She stopped walking. They stood at the railing, the river turning copper below them as the last of the sun hit it at an oblique angle. 'Yes,' she said. 'I want every piece of it exposed and I want every person who made it possible to stand in front of a judge and explain themselves.'

Venn studied her. 'Then I can help you. Comprehensively. But I want immunity. No criminal prosecution. No disbarment. I want protection and I want my name attached to the exposure, not the concealment.'

'You want to be remembered as the man who blew it up,' Elena said.

He didn't flinch. 'I want to be useful before I stop being useful. Yes. That's the honest version.'

Elena looked at him — this precise, methodical man who had spent his career building the very apparatus she was dismantling, and who was now, with the pragmatism of someone reading a balance sheet, deciding it was time to be on the other side of it.

'I can't promise immunity,' she said. 'That's not mine to give. What I can do is ensure your cooperation is documented, genuine, and placed before the court as early as possible. What the court does with that is the court's decision.'

'That's not —'

'It's what I have,' she said. 'Take it or don't.'

He was silent for a long time, the city glittering below them, the river moving with the particular patience of things that have been going in the same direction for longer than any of the people standing on their banks.

'Alright,' he said finally. 'I'll give you an affidavit.'

She walked back to her car alone, the city noise filling the space where the conversation had been. Overhead, a plane tracked north toward the airport, its lights pulsing in the dark.

Her team was waiting. She had a lot to tell them.

## Chapter Ten
## Echoes in the Circuitry

The number seventeen.

Rafiq had been looking at it for forty-eight hours before he understood what it was.

The IP address had first appeared in the server logs in 2017. It pinged Lang's internal archive every Thursday at 2:17 in the morning — not accessing anything, not downloading, just checking, the way a cautious person checks a door is still locked. The pings had continued for six years without triggering a single alert because each one lasted precisely seventeen seconds, which sat below every automated threshold the firm had in place. Someone who understood the system had designed the access pattern for exactly that purpose.

Seventeen minutes. Seventeen seconds. 2017. It had taken Rafiq a day and a half to stop thinking of these as separate numbers and start thinking of them as a signature.

'Someone has had eyes on that archive for six years,' he told Elena and Liz across the kitchen table. 'Not accessing it. Monitoring it. Watching to see if anything moved.'

'To know if anyone was looking,' Elena said.

'Yes.'

'And the memo? Could they see that the memo was still there?'

'A check that granular would require admin-level credentials.' He hesitated. 'The encryption keys used for the 2:17 pings match a pattern I've only seen once before. In the metadata on a document dated 2017, signed with the initials C.M.'

The silence in the kitchen was the silence of people absorbing a confirmation they had been hoping not to need.

'Merrick,' Liz said.

'The patterns match,' Rafiq said carefully. 'I'm not saying she designed it. I'm saying she had access to whatever system generated those keys.'

Liz stood and moved to the window. She stood with her back to the room for a moment, and Elena recognised this as Liz processing something she hadn't decided how to say yet.

'There's something I need to tell you both,' Liz said, without turning. She moved to her bedroom and returned with a battered envelope, which she set on the table. 'My uncle was a city councillor. He resigned in 2001 without explanation. I've had this since he died six years ago. I never opened it fully because —' she paused. 'Because I was afraid of what was in it.'

She spread the contents on the table. Old correspondence, the paper brittle at the edges: letters between her uncle and a law firm — not Lang, but connected — concerning regulatory matters, campaign contributions, and a shell company. The shell company's registration documents were at the bottom of the pile. Its registered agent, in 2001, had been a junior solicitor whose name Elena recognised from a more recent document.

Claudia Merrick.

'This predates everything,' Elena said.

'By at least fifteen years,' Liz said. 'Which means it's not a conflict that arose during this case. It's a relationship that existed long before any of us were involved.'

She told them then about the message that had arrived that morning on her secured work line: Stay quiet or everyone finds out. You know what you owe. She told them calmly, and watched them take it in. 'I'm not going to stay quiet. But you both needed to know it exists.'

Elena looked at her for a moment. 'Thank you for telling us.'

'It changes the strategy,' Liz said.

'It accelerates it,' Elena said. 'Merrick is the judge on our case. If she had prior knowledge of the clause, the concealment of that knowledge is itself grounds for recusal — or worse. We file a sealed disclosure notice. We don't accuse. We ask her to confirm whether she had a prior relationship with the Lang entity, and we document whatever she does with the question.'

The buzzer sounded. They froze in the way of people who have been alert for so long that unexpected sounds have acquired threat levels they don't necessarily deserve.

It was a courier.

The package was small, battered, addressed in handwriting none of them recognised. Inside: a USB stick and a typed note. For Elena. Trust no one. Not even yourselves.

Rafiq scanned the stick immediately. Clean. He opened its contents on the isolated forensic laptop: a single audio file and a collection of deleted emails recovered from Lang's server backup, including a recording of a telephone conversation between Malcolm Venn and a woman whose voice, when they played it, they did not need to hear identified.

'We need to move the timeline,' Elena said.

'We need to move the timeline,' Liz agreed.

Neither of them slept that night. By morning, the sealed disclosure notice had been drafted, reviewed, and filed. The case was no longer approaching a threshold. It had crossed one.

## Chapter Eleven
## The Opening Salvo

The deleted file had a name that Rafiq read aloud with careful neutrality: Clause_14.7_OverrideProtocol_FINAL.docx.

It had been created at 7:42 in the morning on a date Elena recognised. The morning after Daniel Ward's death. It had been accessed twice — once by a user identified as MV, once by CM. It had been deleted at 8:07 on the same morning it was created. Twenty-five minutes from conception to destruction: approximately the same amount of time it takes a human being to panic and then recover enough to act.

'Malcolm Venn,' Rafiq said. 'And Claudia Merrick.'

He set his laptop on the table. The metadata — timestamps, user IDs, access logs, the forensic residue that digital actions leave behind even when the actions themselves have been erased — was displayed with maximum clarity. Not because he expected doubt in this room, but because he had learned, through long experience, that clarity was the only defence against the argument that complexity was the same thing as fabrication.

Liz was already on the phone to Catherine Doyle, their barrister. The call was long. Elena listened to Liz's half of it, filling in Catherine's responses from context and prior knowledge of how Catherine thought. The conclusion: file the metadata as forensic residue, not as a copy of the document. Frame it under Glencore. Don't let the defence characterise it as a document when it was, technically and legally, a shadow — a record that a document existed.

'It's admissible,' Liz said, lowering the phone. 'But they'll fight it. The moment we tender the metadata they'll move to exclude it on grounds of judicial bias — because Merrick's initials are right there in the access log.'

'Which is why we need to file the sealed notice before the trial begins,' Elena said.

'Already drafted,' Liz said.

Maya Torres arrived that morning — a junior attorney Liz had briefed overnight, who walked in with a folder, sharp eyes, and the energy of someone who had been told they were needed urgently and had decided to be equal to that urgency. Her uncle had been injured on a construction site. She did not say this as a justification. She said it as a fact, the way people state facts that have shaped them.

'The access log,' Maya said, after Rafiq walked her through the metadata. 'Twenty-five minutes between creation and deletion. Is there any reading of that that isn't deliberate concealment?'

'There is theoretically always another reading,' Rafiq said. 'The defence will argue document management, clerical error, automated deletion protocols. We have to be ready for each of those.'

'But the user IDs —'

'Are consistent with Venn's and Merrick's system credentials,' Rafiq said. 'Which can be challenged on the grounds that credentials can be shared or misused. We need the testimony to anchor the metadata to the people, not just to the logs.'

They spent the rest of the morning building the case architecture: which pieces of evidence first, in what order, to construct a narrative clear to a jury without sacrificing the forensic precision that would make it unassailable in appeal. The constant negotiation between what was true and what was provable. Between what a jury would understand and what the law required.

Marcus Hall called in the afternoon. 'They've reassigned me. Remote compliance audit. No access to litigation files.'

'They're trying to isolate you before the trial,' Elena said.

'I assumed as much.' A pause. 'It doesn't change my intention to testify.'

'I know. But Marcus — are you secure?'

'I have copies of everything at three separate locations, none of them accessible through the firm's systems.' Another pause, longer. 'I did this correctly. I was just — I did this much too late.'

'You're doing it now,' Elena said. 'That's what matters.'

Monday was two days away. The trial bundle was assembled, reviewed, and certified. The sealed notice had been filed that afternoon and acknowledged by the court registry with the minimum of procedural language that gave nothing away.

That evening, Catherine Doyle called Elena directly. Her voice was precise and unhurried, but beneath the precision was something that might, in a less disciplined person, have been excitement.

'They've filed a last-minute motion,' she said. 'Application to exclude all metadata evidence on grounds of judicial bias and procedural unfairness. Before the trial has even started.'

'What does that tell us?' Elena asked.

'That they've seen our sealed notice and they're rattled,' Catherine said. 'And that they believe we have more than we've disclosed. They're not just defending. They're afraid.' A brief pause. 'Monday. I'll see you Monday.'

## Chapter Twelve
## The Metadata Reckoning

The room had the stillness of people waiting on something that is almost certainly about to happen but hasn't happened yet. Rafiq's laptop sat open on the table, its forensic dashboard displayed. Elena stood at the window. Liz sat with her hands folded in a way that suggested she had been deliberately keeping them still for some time.

'There,' Rafiq said.

He pointed. On the screen: a single folder in a recovered state, the timestamp and access logs Elena already knew. Below those, the user IDs. Below those, the key pattern analysis linking the access to the credentials associated with the two names they had been working toward for weeks.

The document's name hovered at the top of the display: Clause_14.7_OverrideProtocol_FINAL.docx. Created. Accessed. Deleted. Twenty-five minutes that someone had decided were enough to contain a truth.

They had not been enough.

'The metadata is not the document,' Rafiq said, for the fourth time in as many days. 'It is forensic residue. It is evidence that the document existed, that specific individuals accessed it, and that it was deleted in circumstances consistent with intentional concealment. What the document said — that we do not have. What it was used for — that we can infer, and that Venn's affidavit will confirm.'

'The defence will argue inference isn't proof,' Liz said.

'Inference is always the mechanism by which intent is established,' Rafiq said mildly. 'The defence's own case will rely on inference. They'll infer that our witnesses have motives to fabricate. Inference cuts both ways.'

Elena looked at the screen. Looked at the names. Thought about Merrick — the judge assigned to their case, whose initials appeared in a metadata record describing a document created the morning after Daniel died and deleted twenty-five minutes later.

'We file the sealed notice this afternoon,' she said.

The notice was a model of legal restraint: it did not accuse Justice Merrick of anything. It asked her, through the proper procedural channel, to confirm whether she had had a prior professional relationship with the Lang entity, and whether that relationship had involved any work relating to the contractual provisions now at issue in the proceedings. Careful, precise, and as neutrally worded as a document containing a live grenade could be.

The court registry acknowledged receipt at 4:47 PM.

Justice Merrick's response arrived the following morning, three lines on official court letterhead: The Court acknowledges receipt of the sealed notice. The matter will be addressed at the commencement of trial. No admission. No denial. A holding position.

'She's buying time,' Elena said.

'Or she's genuinely uncertain about her exposure and taking advice,' Liz said. 'Either way she's not going to make this easy.'

Catherine Doyle had reviewed the response and delivered her assessment over the phone with characteristic brevity: proceed to trial. The sealed notice was on record. Her non-response was itself part of the record. If she ruled against them on the metadata motion and they appealed, they had everything they needed.

The trial was five days away. The team ran through witness preparation in two long sessions. Gareth in the morning, Marcus in the afternoon, with Rafiq available throughout for forensic questions the witnesses might be asked and needed to understand. Elena observed, made notes, asked the cross-examination questions she expected Amira Chen to ask, and watched the witnesses become, over the course of the sessions, more composed and more precise.

On the fourth evening before trial, Elena sat alone at her kitchen table and read through the case from the beginning. All of it. Every document, every statement, every piece of evidence in the order in which it would be presented.

It was a strong case. The strongest she had ever built. And she had built it out of a clause in a contract that nobody had thought to look at, and a photograph of her brother in a hard hat, and the particular quality of attention she had always had for the things other people decided were routine.

She thought about Daniel's voice on the recording.

Don't be careful. Be right.

She was going to court on Monday.

Chapter Thirteen
## Day One

*Monday, 1 July — Supreme Court of Queensland, Courtroom 7B*

The media had gathered outside on the courthouse concourse before seven. Elena walked past them with Catherine Doyle at her side, saying nothing, looking at nothing except the entrance directly ahead. Liz was two steps behind, carrying the trial bundle as though it were something precious — which it was.

Courtroom 7B was large and formal and filled to its gallery capacity. Construction workers, many of them — some in work clothes they had come straight from the site in, some in the neat, uncomfortable dress of people who don't often wear it. Union representatives. Legal observers. Three rows of journalists. Elena recognised some faces from the days following Thursday's publication. Others were new, drawn by the story's expansion over the weekend.

She took her place at the plaintiffs' table beside Liz, Gareth, and Marcus. Across the aisle, Fortis Constructions' retained counsel, Geoffrey Langford, organised his papers with the unhurried ease of a man who had appeared in this courtroom many times and considered it familiar territory. Amira Chen from Lang & Associates sat beside him, composure precise, expression giving nothing away.

The Court Officer called the matter. Justice Claudia Merrick entered.

She was sixty-one, silver-haired, with the bearing of a person accustomed to having rooms recalibrate around her arrival. She surveyed the courtroom briefly before taking her seat, and Elena, watching, saw nothing in her expression to indicate that today was anything other than a standard Monday.

Either she was very good at this, or she had resolved the question of her prior involvement to her own satisfaction. Elena made a note and set it aside.

Catherine Doyle rose for the opening.

'May it please the Court. This case concerns the deliberate concealment of safety violations through a contractual mechanism known as Clause 14.7, inserted into construction contracts over a period of approximately seven years.' Her voice was measured, her pace unhurried — the cadence of someone who has enough time for the truth. 'The plaintiffs will demonstrate that this clause was not a drafting anomaly or an oversight. It was a strategic device, conceived, implemented, and protected by the defendants, whose purpose was to delay mandatory safety inspections and shift legal liability to parties with fewer resources to defend themselves.'

She paused — a deliberate pause, the kind that invites a courtroom to sit with a sentence before moving past it.

'We will tender evidence from whistleblowers, forensic analysts, and internal witnesses. We will establish that Lang & Associates designed and supplied the legal architecture for concealment, and that Fortis Constructions deployed it with fatal consequences. We will demonstrate a pattern of conduct that cannot be explained by negligence or oversight, but only by intent.' Another pause. 'The plaintiffs do not seek vengeance. They seek accountability. And the evidence will show they are entitled to it.'

The courtroom was quiet as she sat.

Amira Chen stood with a composure that Elena found, despite herself, professionally admirable. 'Your Honour, the defendants deny all allegations. Clause 14.7 was a standard contractual provision, reviewed and approved in accordance with ordinary industry practice. The plaintiffs' case rests on speculation, hearsay, and evidence whose admissibility is itself in question.'

She gestured toward the plaintiffs' table with controlled precision. 'The tragic death of Mr. Daniel Ward was fully investigated and found to be accidental. The plaintiffs now seek to relitigate a settled matter through litigation that depends on documents of disputed provenance and witnesses with clear personal motivation. The defendants will demonstrate that at every stage, Lang & Associates acted within its professional obligations and that Fortis Constructions followed lawful advice.'

She sat.

Justice Merrick looked between the two parties with an expression that gave nothing away. 'Thank you. The plaintiffs will tender their initial affidavits.'

Catherine stood again and began. Five affidavits: Elena's investigative chronology, Marcus's ethics committee documentation, Gareth's whistleblower statement, Rafiq's forensic analysis, Liz's media coordination record. Each one received and marked in turn.

Then Amira Chen stood again.

'Your Honour. Before evidence is heard, the defendants seek to move a preliminary application. We seek to exclude all metadata evidence relating to the Clause_14.7_OverrideProtocol_FINAL.docx on three grounds. First, judicial bias — the alleged access by Your Honour to the document creates a perception of conflict that cannot be managed through a sealed notice. Second, procedural unfairness — the document was not disclosed through the standard discovery process. Third, privilege — the document was created within a legally privileged professional context.'

Justice Merrick's expression did not change. 'Ms Chen, are you alleging bias against this Court?'

A slight pause. 'We raise it as a matter of procedural integrity, Your Honour.'

Catherine was on her feet. 'Your Honour, the metadata is not the document. It is forensic residue — a record of actions taken, not a reproduction of content. It was not concealed in discovery because it was not known to exist until forensic recovery. And it is admissible as lawfully obtained digital evidence under the principles confirmed in Glencore International AG v Commissioner of Taxation.'

Justice Merrick looked at the two barristers for a long moment. 'I will hear full argument on the preliminary application tomorrow morning. The trial will proceed in parallel.'

As the afternoon session began — Gareth Lin called to the stand, Catherine guiding him carefully through his statement, Amira's cross-examination following with the systematic patience of someone dismantling a structure they believe will eventually fall — Elena sat at the plaintiffs' table and kept her breathing steady.

She was here. The case was here.

In the corridor during the afternoon recess, her phone showed a message from Catherine: Prepare for cross. Tomorrow, they go after you. Hard.

Elena put the phone away. She was ready.

## Chapter Fourteen
## **Crossfire**

Amira Chen had a particular way of beginning a cross-examination: she would establish a premise so reasonable, so apparently well-disposed toward the witness, that the witness relaxed into it before understanding where it was leading. Elena had watched it from across the aisle. Now she was on the receiving end of it, and she was not going to relax.

Catherine had prepared her for two hours the previous evening. 'She'll start with Daniel,' Catherine had said. 'She'll be compassionate. She'll invite you to agree that you loved him, that his death changed you. All of which is true. And then she'll use those agreements to argue that everything you've done since is emotional rather than factual.'

'I know,' Elena had said.

'Know it again on the stand, in real time, under oath, while a courtroom full of people watches you feel it.'

Elena took the oath. She sat. She placed her hands on the edge of the witness box and kept them still.

'Ms Ward,' Amira began, her voice at its warmest. 'Your brother Daniel died in 2019. He was thirty-seven years old.'

'Thirty-seven, yes.'

'You were very close.'

'We were.'

'His death was a profound loss.'

'Yes.'

'And it was that loss that led you, two years later, to the document review that identified Clause 14.7.'

Elena paused — just slightly. 'My professional judgment identified Clause 14.7. The clause is irregular. That irregularity is what drew my attention.'

'But you were reviewing documents for a minor residential matter,' Amira said pleasantly. 'It was late. You were alone. And you found a clause that you then connected to Fortis Constructions — the same company on whose site your brother died.'

'The clause connected itself to Fortis Constructions,' Elena said. 'It appeared in three of their contracts. I observed the pattern. That's what I was in the room to do.'

'Of course.' Amira shifted smoothly. 'Let me ask you directly: did your personal connection to Fortis Constructions influence the significance you attributed to Clause 14.7?'

'No. The significance of the clause is objective. It appears in multiple contracts. It is linguistically irregular. The buildings associated with those contracts reported structural failures. The significance of those facts is not altered by my personal history.'

'But your motivation to pursue them —'

'My motivation is irrelevant to their truth,' Elena said. 'Investigators are frequently motivated by personal experience. Motivation and integrity are not the same variable.'

Amira moved on. The coordination with the media. The arrangement with Gareth. The nature of the relationship — a word Amira used with careful ambiguity — between Elena and the three whistleblowers whose statements formed the core of the case.

Elena answered each question with the precision she had spent two years developing: specific without elaboration, without the over-explanation that sounds defensive, without the brevity that sounds evasive. She had learned this from Catherine, who had been teaching her, in the weeks before trial, how to occupy a witness box correctly.

'Ms Ward,' Amira said, near the end, 'you cannot speak for your brother. He is not here. His fears, as you've described them, are not evidence.'

Elena looked at her steadily. 'Daniel's recordings are evidence. His documented safety complaints, which were received and suppressed, are evidence. The metadata showing that a document describing how to isolate Lang from liability was created the morning after he died — that is evidence.' A pause. 'I am not presenting my brother's fears. I am presenting the record that those fears were justified.'

In the gallery, one of the jurors — a woman in her fifties who had been leaning forward slightly for most of the session — sat back with a small, private nod.

Elena did not look at her. She had been told never to look at the jury during cross-examination, and she was not going to look at the jury during cross-examination.

She stepped down. Catherine met her at the bar table with an expression of precisely calibrated restraint.

'Good,' Catherine said quietly. 'That was very good.'

Elena sat, and concentrated on keeping her breathing regular, and did not let herself feel anything about it until later, alone, when there was time.

## Chapter Fifteen
## The Whistleblower

Marcus Hall took the stand on the third morning of trial, and the courtroom understood immediately that what it was watching was not a performance. He was composed in the way of someone who has been preparing for a long time and has accepted, somewhere between preparation and this room, that composure was the only form of courage available to him.

Catherine led him through it carefully.

He had been a senior associate at Lang & Associates for eleven years. He had served on the firm's internal ethics committee for six. In 2018, reviewing a subcontractor agreement for a Fortis Constructions project, he had identified Clause 14.7 as an anomaly. He had escalated his concern, in writing, to the ethics committee. He had been told — verbally, in a meeting whose minutes he had noted separately, in a personal document stored offsite — that the clause represented 'strategic risk management' and that he should not pursue it further.

'Did you document that instruction?' Catherine asked.

'Yes. I wrote a personal memo the same afternoon and stored it separately from the firm's systems.'

'Why separately?'

A pause. 'Because I was concerned that documents on the firm's systems might not remain there.' He said this without emphasis. It landed like a very heavy thing placed very carefully on a glass surface.

'And when you subsequently learned that Clause 14.7 had been present on the site where Daniel Ward died?'

'I began collecting internal records. I was not certain at the time whether the clause had caused the accident or whether it had simply failed to prevent it. I understood, however, that the distinction mattered less than the question of why the clause existed at all.'

'And why did it exist?'

Marcus was quiet for a moment — not hesitating, thinking. 'Because it was profitable. And because the people who designed it believed that the legal exposure it created could be managed. That the inspections would happen eventually. That any incident that occurred in the interim could be settled quietly.' He paused. 'They were right about most of that. What they didn't account for was someone refusing to let it be settled quietly.'

He did not look at Elena when he said this. He didn't need to.

Amira Chen's cross-examination was, Elena thought, her best work of the trial — and also, paradoxically, her most revealing. She established Marcus's career stagnation. She produced an ethics committee evaluation that characterised him as 'inflexible' and resistant to 'strategic objectives.' She implied, with exquisite precision, that a man who had spent eleven years failing to advance was a man with reasons to damage the institution that had failed to reward him.

Marcus let her finish. Then he said: 'I raised ethical concerns. That wasn't popular. I remained in my role because I chose to remain — because I believed that someone with my knowledge of the firm's practices should stay proximate to those practices and document what happened.' He looked at Amira with the steady attention of someone who is not impressed by cleverness when truth is available. 'I am not testifying because I am resentful. I am testifying because Daniel Ward is dead and I knew, before he died, that the conditions which killed him were preventable. That is something I have to live with. This testimony is part of how I do that.'

The courtroom was quiet.

During the lunch recess, Catherine sat with Elena and Liz in a small conference room. 'They're trying to make this about character because they can't make it about facts,' she said. 'The facts don't support them. Their only strategy is to make the jury doubt the people presenting the facts. We stay on evidence. We let the evidence accumulate.'

Liz nodded. 'They're rattled. You can see it in the way Chen's pacing her cross. She's going longer than she needs to on each witness because she's hoping something unexpected will surface. Nothing unexpected is going to surface.'

'Unless we put it there ourselves,' Elena said.

Liz looked at her.

'Venn's affidavit,' Elena said. 'Catherine — when does it land?'

Catherine's expression was very still for a moment. Then: 'Tomorrow morning. Seven forty-two. Hand-delivered to the registry. I'll be in early.'

## Chapter Sixteen
**The Technician**

Rafiq Mehta took the stand on the afternoon of the third day, and the defence made the mistake of assuming that a man who spent his days inside computers would be uncomfortable under cross-examination.

He was not uncomfortable. He was, if anything, slightly relieved — the way a person is relieved to finally explain something they have been waiting to explain for a long time.

Catherine walked him through the forensic timeline with the methodical patience of someone presenting something genuinely important to people who will need it explained properly: the metadata, what it was, what it showed, what it meant, and why the absence of the document itself did not diminish the evidential significance of its ghost.

'The metadata is not the document,' he said, at one point. 'An analogy: if I visit a house and leave fingerprints, those fingerprints do not contain the contents of my visit. But they establish that I was there, when I was there, and what I touched. That is what the metadata establishes here. Not what the document said. That specific users, at specific times, performed specific actions with a file that was subsequently deleted.'

'And what do those actions indicate?' Catherine asked.

'The creation timestamp — 7:42 in the morning, the day after Daniel Ward's death — indicates the document was created in close temporal proximity to the event it purported to address. First access by MV four minutes after creation. Second access by CM eleven minutes after the first. Deletion eight minutes after the second access.' He paused. 'The total lifecycle of this document was twenty-five minutes. In my professional experience, documents are deleted within twenty-five minutes of creation when their creators determine, after reviewing them, that the risk of their existence outweighs their utility.'

Amira Chen's cross-examination lasted forty minutes and accomplished, Elena thought, slightly less than Amira had intended.

She established that access logs could theoretically be manipulated. Rafiq acknowledged this and explained, methodically and without irritation, why the specific patterns were inconsistent with that hypothesis. She established that deletion could occur in the normal course of document management. Rafiq acknowledged this and explained, methodically and without irritation, why a document created, reviewed by two senior-level users, and deleted within twenty-five minutes was not consistent with normal practice. She established that Rafiq was employed by the plaintiffs. Rafiq acknowledged this and noted, mildly, that the defence's own experts were also employed by interested parties.

'The data,' he said, in response to Amira's final question, 'is what it is. I am telling you what it shows. Whether you find that telling convenient or inconvenient is not a variable in the analysis.'

In the gallery, two jurors were writing.

After the session, Mia Torres sent Elena a message with four names attached. Three were willing to testify. One was willing to testify to something that Mia said Elena should know about immediately.

Elena called her back.

The former employee was Rachel Mitchell. She had worked directly under Malcolm Venn. She had been present in meetings where Clause 14.7 had been discussed not as an industry standard but as a solution to a problem — the problem of liability, the problem of inspection schedules, the problem of what happens when a project's financials require corners to be cut and the law requires those corners to be rounded.

'She's willing to testify?' Elena said.

'She's been waiting to testify for three years,' Mia said. 'She just needed someone to ask.'

Elena stared at the ceiling of the courthouse corridor and felt the particular sensation of a case becoming what it always had the potential to become.

'Get her to Catherine tonight,' she said. 'We need her on the stand before the end of the week.'

## Chapter Seventeen
## **The Collapse**

*Day Four — 7:42 AM*

The affidavit arrived in a sealed envelope, hand-delivered to the court registry before the building was fully open, with the words Urgent – Disclosure Statement on the outer cover in block letters that managed to be both precise and grave.

Catherine Doyle read it in the corridor outside Courtroom 7B, standing very still, turning pages with the focused attention of someone reading not for comprehension but for consequence.

Elena watched her.

'It's real,' Catherine said finally, without looking up. 'And it's comprehensive.'

The affidavit was fourteen pages, sworn and signed by Malcolm Venn, setting out — in the unhurried, carefully structured language of a man who had spent his career building arguments and was now, for the first time, building one against himself — the full history of Clause 14.7.

He had conceived it. He had designed the language, tested it against relevant statutory provisions, and confirmed that it sat, within a narrow margin of legal interpretation, just outside the range of provisions that would trigger mandatory disclosure to regulators. He had briefed the senior partners. He had managed the deployment across multiple projects over six years.

He had created, the morning after Daniel Ward's death, a document outlining the strategy for isolating Lang from liability in the event that the clause was challenged — and he had shared it with Claudia Merrick, then a compliance consultant, who had reviewed it and suggested two amendments before it was deleted.

He was prepared to testify. He requested immunity from professional sanctions and from criminal prosecution for conduct disclosed in the affidavit.

At nine o'clock, Catherine tendered the affidavit to the court.

Justice Merrick received it without expression, read the first two pages, set it down, and requested a two-hour adjournment.

Outside the courtroom, Lang's legal team moved with the contained urgency of people who had been expecting something bad and had discovered that what arrived was worse. Elena watched from across the corridor as Amira Chen conducted a rapid, quiet conversation on her phone with someone who appeared to be providing instructions she was not entirely comfortable receiving.

Geoffrey Langford crossed the corridor and approached the plaintiffs' team.

'Private meeting,' he said. 'To discuss the implications of the affidavit.'

Liz stepped forward before Elena could speak. 'No.'

'This changes the landscape significantly for both parties —'

'The landscape has changed in one direction,' Liz said. 'We're not interested in helping you redecorate.'

Langford looked at Elena. Elena said nothing. He returned across the corridor.

By ten-thirty, Lang & Associates had filed a Notice of Intention to Amend the Defence, attempting to characterise Venn's conduct as unauthorised and undisclosed to the partnership. Fortis Constructions filed a Security for Costs Application arguing the case had changed materially since their initial legal position was established.

Catherine responded to both within the hour. 'The affidavit is sworn. The admissions are the defendant's own senior partner's. "We didn't know" is not a defence to "our most senior partner did it."'

At eleven o'clock, Justice Merrick reconvened the court. Her expression, Elena thought, had changed — not in the way a guilty person's expression changes, but in the way a professional's does when they are managing the distance between what has happened and what is required of them.

'The affidavit of Mr Venn is received and marked,' she said. 'The Court acknowledges the gravity of the admissions made and their direct relevance to the pleaded issues.' She paused, in the way of someone who has thought carefully about the next sentence. 'The Court also notes the reference to my prior consultancy role. I confirm that in 2017, I provided limited compliance advice to the Lang entity. I did not draft or approve Clause 14.7, nor was I aware of its deployment at the time of that advice. I did not access the Override Protocol document with any understanding of its significance, and my access predated my judicial appointment by four years.'

Complete silence in the courtroom.

'I will not recuse myself. I will continue to preside. Any formal challenge to my impartiality must be made through the proper procedural channel.' She looked at Catherine, then at Amira Chen. 'We will proceed.'

Catherine said, quietly: 'We reserve our position.'

Lang and Fortis, for the first time since the trial began, looked like two different parties rather than a coordinated defence. A shift in the physical arrangement of their legal teams; the body language of consultation becoming, over the past hour, the body language of separation.

The walls were cracking.

That evening, Catherine forwarded Elena a message: Lang is preparing to settle. Fortis is resisting. They're dividing. Attached was a draft settlement proposal headed Confidential – Without Admission of Liability.

Elena read it. Then she called Catherine back. 'What do you want to do?' Catherine asked.

'I want to finish it,' Elena said.

Chapter Eighteen

## The Reckoning

The settlement offer arrived in a sealed envelope before court resumed: Confidential Settlement Proposal – Without Admission of Liability. Elena read it in the mediation suite with Catherine on one side and Liz on the other.

Four point two milFortis dollars. Non-disparagement. No admission of wrongdoing. Withdrawal of all claims against Lang. Full confidentiality.

The figure was not insulting. That was, in a way, the most insulting thing about it.

'They've done the calculation,' Liz said, reading over her shoulder. 'They know what a public judgment costs versus a private settlement. They've decided four milFortis is cheaper than the trial record.'

'And quieter,' Gareth said from the corner. He had been quiet since arriving that morning. 'They're asking us to take the money and disappear. It's what they've always wanted. It's what they tried to achieve with Daniel's settlement. Paid, quiet, gone.'

Elena set the document on the table. 'We reject it.'

'Elena —' Catherine began, in the tone of a barrister who wants to ensure her client has considered all dimensions.

'We reject it publicly,' Elena said. 'On the record. I want it in the transcript that we were offered this and we declined.' She looked around the room: Liz, nodding slowly; Marcus, hands folded, expression set; Gareth, who looked, for the first time that morning, less burdened. 'This is not about the money. This was never about the money. If we settle, they settle. They pay the fine and the clause keeps existing. Other firms keep using variations of it. Other people die. We're not settling.'

Catherine looked at her for a moment. Then she stood, collected her papers. 'Alright. We go back in.'

Back in Courtroom 7B, Catherine rose before Justice Merrick could call the proceedings to order.

'Your Honour, the plaintiffs confirm receipt of a confidential settlement offer from Lang & Associates, received this morning. We respectfully decline.' A pause. 'We believe the public interest in the matter before this Court outweighs any private resolution, and we proceed on that basis.'

Justice Merrick received this without visible reaction. 'Proceed to closing submissions.'

Catherine's closing was twenty-four minutes. She did not raise her voice. She did not use rhetorical flourishes. She presented the evidence — clause by clause, document by document, witness by witness — in the order in which it had been heard and described in plain language what each piece established and what it meant when assembled together.

'The defendants,' she said, near the end, 'ask this Court to believe that what happened here was a series of oversights, coincidences, and failures of communication. The evidence does not support that account. A clause was designed, deployed, and defended. A document was created and deleted. Concerns were raised and suppressed. A man died and a settlement was arranged. These things did not happen by accident. They happened because a system existed that made each of them possible, and because the people who benefited from that system had the resources to keep it running quietly.'

She paused.

'The plaintiffs do not ask for vengeance. They ask for an account that names what happened accurately. For Daniel Ward. For every worker who stood on a site where an inspection had been deferred because a clause said it could be. For every family that accepted a settlement payment without knowing what had been bought and sold alongside it.' She turned to face the bench directly. 'We ask this Court to find that Clause 14.7 was a breach of the duty of care owed to every person who worked under it. That its concealment was deliberate. That the people responsible for it are accountable. And that justice, in this matter, must be public.'

She sat.

The room was very still.

## Chapter Nineteen
## The Respondents' Stand

The defence case unfolded across three days with the careful dignity of people who had stopped believing they could win and were now concentrating on how much they could limit.

Jonathan Reeve led for Lang, calling first Dr Felix Wainwright — the firm's head of compliance — to establish a narrative of institutional diligence. Wainwright was precise, well-prepared, and gave the impression of a man who had reviewed his own institution's practices with genuine thoroughness and arrived, honestly, at the conclusion that things had been handled well. He was, Elena thought, probably not lying. He probably did believe what he was saying. That was what made him, under cross-examination, the defence's most damaging witness.

Catherine produced Exhibit 42: an internal correspondence chain from 2018, documenting a safety concern about a Fortis Constructions project that had been reviewed, noted, and filed without response. The chain had run to seven emails across four months. It had not been escalated. No action had been taken.

'Dr Wainwright, you testified that due diligence protocols require escalation of unanswered safety concerns within thirty days.'

'Correct.'

'Can you explain to the Court why this concern, spanning four months and seven emails, was not escalated?'

Wainwright looked at the exhibit for a long moment. 'I cannot explain that' he said. 'That should have been escalated.'

'Thank you,' Catherine said, and sat down.

Fortis's CEO, Marcus Cheung, took the stand the following morning with the self-possession of a man accustomed to rooms that arranged themselves around his authority. He described transparency as a core value. He described their relationship with regulatory bodies as collaborative. He described the deployment of Clause 14.7 as consistent with industry practice and as having been reviewed by external legal counsel whose advice he had relied upon.

'External legal counsel,' Catherine noted during cross. 'Being Lang & Associates.'

'Among others.'

'And when Lang & Associates advised you that Clause 14.7 was consistent with your statutory obligations, did you conduct an independent review of that advice?'

A fractional pause. 'We relied on our legal advisers.'

'Mr Cheung, are you aware that one of your legal advisers has now sworn an affidavit stating that the clause was specifically designed to delay mandatory safety inspections?'

'I am aware of the affidavit.'

'Does that change your characterisation of the advice as legally sound?'

The silence lasted four seconds. In a courtroom, four seconds is a very long time.

'That is a matter for the Court,' Cheung said finally.

The defence's most precisely constructed witness was Mira Gallagher, an independent risk management consultant brought in to provide expert evidence that Fortis's practices were consistent with industry standards. Her credentials were impeccable. Her testimony was thorough. She made one mistake.

Catherine introduced, during cross-examination, a confidential report Gallagher had authored eight months earlier, commissioned by a Fortis industry body and never publicly released. In it, Gallagher had identified what she described as 'systemic blind spots' in the construction industry's approach to subcontractor safety obligations. She had recommended regulatory review.

'Ms Gallagher, you authored this report?'

'I did.'

'And the systemic blind spots you identified — were they identified in the context of clauses that defer or limit inspection obligations?'

A long pause. 'Among other contexts, yes.'

'Thank you.'

The final witness was Rowan Malik, a junior analyst from Fortis's compliance division. He was twenty-six and nervous in the way of someone who has been told what to say and is concentrating so hard on saying it that he has not considered the questions he might be asked. Then Catherine asked him one.

'Mr Malik, in your experience as a compliance analyst, have you ever received instructions to expedite due diligence steps in order to meet executive project targets?'

He answered without thinking, which was the last honest thing he had expected to do in this room: 'Yes.'

A ripple went through the gallery.

'Thank you,' Catherine said. 'Nothing further.'

The respondents' case closed the following afternoon. In the boardroom of Lang & Associates that evening, one partner said to another, in the tone of a conclusion that has been reached but not yet spoken aloud: 'We won't win.'

No one argued.

## Chapter Twenty
## **Judgment Reserved**

The city moved with its ordinary indifference through the two days of deliberation, as though the question of accountability for a dead man and a buried clause was a matter to be resolved on a schedule it had no stake in.

Elena spent most of those two days at her own desk for the first time in weeks — working on other files, returning calls that had accumulated during the trial, trying to occupy the ordinary texture of professional life while waiting for a judgment that would either confirm the past two years had been moving toward something real, or instruct her, in precise legal language, to begin the process of reassessment.

She did not think about it more than she could help.

Liz had taken a different approach, which was to think about it constantly and systematically: running through scenarios, preparing the team's response to each possible outcome, drafting the press statement for the judgment Elena was hoping for and a careful, separate response for the one she wasn't.

Gareth had gone to his sister's house in Toowoomba. He had sent a single message: I've done what I can. The rest is the court's. Let me know.

Marcus Hall had remained in Brisbane, in the small apartment he had been staying in since his effective removal from the firm, reading. She did not ask what he was reading. She thought it was probably not legal texts.

The judgment was delivered on a Thursday morning to a courtroom that was, if anything, fuller than it had been on day one. Additional gallery seats had been arranged. The media contingent had expanded. Several of the construction workers from the opening days were back — some in the same work clothes, all of them carrying the particular stillness of people who have been told their story is being told and are waiting to learn how it ends.

Justice Merrick entered. She read for twenty-two minutes. The courtroom listened.

'The Court finds that Clause 14.7 was designed to delay mandatory safety inspections and deflect liability. The evidence demonstrates beyond the required standard that Lang & Associates knowingly facilitated its deployment, and that its senior partnership was aware of both its purpose and its consequences.'

A held breath across the gallery.

'The Court further finds that Fortis Constructions acted on this advice, resulting in systemic breaches of its statutory duty of care under the Work Health and Safety Act, which breaches contributed directly to the conditions in which Daniel Ward died.'

Elena closed her eyes.

'The plaintiffs are awarded damages in the amount of six point eight milFortis dollars, inclusive of costs.'

Beside her, Liz made a small, contained sound that was not quite a gasp and not quite a word but was, unmistakably, relief.

'The Court refers the conduct of Lang & Associates to the Legal Services Commission for review. The Court refers the conduct of Fortis Constructions to the Queensland Building and Construction Commission. The Court refers the prior consultancy of Justice Merrick to the Judicial Commission for review in accordance with the provisions of the Judicial Commission Act.'

She set down the judgment. 'That concludes the Court's findings.'

As she rose and the courtroom rose with her, the sound in the gallery changed — from silence to something that moved through the rows of construction workers and their families like air released from a long-held position. Not cheering. Something more considered than cheering.

On the courthouse steps, cameras and microphones and questions. Elena stood beside Catherine and Liz and chose her words carefully, because what she said now was part of the record, and the record was what would outlast all of them.

'Today is an important day for every worker in this industry,' she said. 'It is also not enough on its own. Accountability in a courtroom is the beginning of change, not the end of it. We will continue.'

She stepped back from the microphones.

Her phone contained a message from Fortis Constructions' general counsel: Notice of Appeal – served as of 11:32 AM.

Liz, reading over her shoulder, said: 'Good. Let them appeal.'

Elena put the phone in her pocket and looked out at the city. The river. The bridges. The ordinary morning machinery of Brisbane going about its day.

The fight was not over. She had known, walking in, that it wouldn't be. She had won the thing that was available to be won today. Tomorrow's fight was tomorrow's.

## Chapter Twenty-One
# The Veil Breaks

The appeal was broad, as Elena had anticipated. Fortis Constructions challenged the admissibility of the metadata evidence, the credibility of the whistleblower testimony, the finding of causation, and the quantum of damages. Lang & Associates had joined the appeal in part, seeking to excise the finding of intentional concealment.

The Queensland Court of Appeal was more austere than the trial court — higher ceilings, less gallery, a bench of three. Justice Elisa Carr presided, flanked by two associate judges whose expressions during Fortis's opening submissions conveyed attentiveness without encouragement.

Geoffrey Langford opened for Fortis with precision: the metadata was forensic residue without proper foundation; the timeline was interpretive rather than evidentiary; the finding of intent was speculative where it should have been proven.

Catherine responded with the composed certainty of a barrister who has been here before and does not find the altitude disorienting. She cited Glencore. She cited the authentication process, the chain of custody, Rafiq's methodology. She walked the bench through the structural argument for why the trial judge's findings on causation were not only open but compelled by the evidence.

During the morning recess, Elena's secured device received a message from an encrypted address she didn't recognise.

*'I worked at Fortis. I saw the memos. They knew the Southbridge site was unstable. They sabotaged the inspection schedule.'*

The sender identified himself as K. Doyle, former site engineer. Attached was a document dated March 2019: Fortis Internal – Site Risk Memo. Subject line: Delay inspection. Avoid audit. Risk acceptable. Signed by a senior Fortis executive.

Elena forwarded it to Catherine immediately: This changes everything.

It did.

That evening, The Signal published what its editors had chosen to describe, with some understatement, as a significant development. The leaked email chain from 2017 — Claudia Merrick to the Lang ethics committee, subject line Clause 14.7 – Strategic Risk Language — was reproduced in full. The critical sentence: Ensure the clause is insulated from statutory triggers. Delay is defensible if framed as procedural.

By morning, the Judicial Commission had announced an accelerated inquiry. The Premier had issued a statement. The minister formerly responsible for building safety regulation, Hon. Peter Halstead, was named in three separate documents as having received briefings from Lang's legal team concerning 'contractual insulation frameworks.'

Halstead resigned within forty-eight hours.

Back in the appeal court, Justice Carr received Catherine's application to tender the Doyle memo as fresh evidence. The standard was high — fresh evidence on appeal required compelling justification — and

Catherine met it: the evidence could not have been obtained with reasonable diligence before trial; it directly contradicted the factual foundation of Fortis's appeal grounds; its credibility was capable of assessment on its face. Justice Carr admitted it, provisionally, pending verification.

Lang's legal team — watching Fortis's case deteriorate around the newly admitted memo — withdrew from the appeal entirely that afternoon. They issued a brief statement: Lang & Associates accepts the trial court's findings and will cooperate fully with all regulatory reviews.

Fortis stood alone.

Elena turned to Liz in the corridor. 'The veil is breaking.'

Liz nodded, watching Fortis's counsel confer in urgent, unhappy whispers across the hall. 'It already has.'

## Chapter Twenty-Two
## The Testimony

Kieran Doyle entered the appellate courtroom flanked by whistleblower protection officers. His plain suit did little to mask the tension in his posture, but determination was legible in his face — the particular set of a person who has been waiting a long time to say something and has finally arrived at the room where saying it will count.

Catherine introduced him with the careful formality that fresh evidence on appeal required: the application for leave, the grounds of relevance, the reasons why this testimony was not available at trial. Justice Carr, over the vehement objections of Fortis's counsel, nodded once. 'Proceed.'

Kieran took the stand. He adjusted his collar, looked at the bench, and began.

'I worked on the Southbridge Tower project. I was present during internal meetings where Clause 14.7 was discussed.'

A silence fell over the courtroom — the specific silence of people sensing that what comes next will matter.

'We were told to delay inspections. Not because of scheduling. Because the site was not ready. There were structural issues — cracks in the load-bearing columns. When I raised concerns, I was told: "Clause 14.7 protects us. Delay is legal."'

He paused. 'After Daniel Ward filed his report, I saw a memo. It said: Audit flagged. Delay protocol active. Risk acceptable. That memo was signed by a senior Fortis executive.'

He handed up the document. Justice Carr examined it. Passed it to the associate judges. A long moment.

Fortis's counsel, Langford, stood. 'Mr Doyle, you left Fortis under a cloud, didn't you?'

'I resigned after being threatened.'

'You never reported these concerns to regulators?'

'I tried. I was ignored.'

'So you come forward now — during an appeal?'

'Because now someone's listening,' Kieran said.

Langford sat down.

Justice Carr looked at the document for a long moment before she spoke. 'The Court accepts Mr Doyle's testimony. The memo will be admitted into evidence.'

• • •

That afternoon, Parliament convened an emergency session. The inquiry into regulatory failures expanded rapidly. Minister Halstead was summoned. As the session progressed, the Premier rose: 'This government will not protect those who enabled corporate negligence. The inquiry will have full powers.'

Halstead's resignation was confirmed within forty-eight hours.

Back in court, Justice Carr denied Fortis's application for a stay of proceedings. 'The appeal will proceed. The Court will deliver judgment next week.'

The following day, Elena held a press conference outside the courthouse with Catherine, Liz, and — for the first time in public, without sunglasses — Kieran Doyle.

'Today marks a crucial turning point,' Catherine said. 'Kieran Doyle's testimony confirmed what we have long known: that negligence was not a failure. It was a practice.'

Elena stepped forward. She held up a copy of the site risk memo — Risk acceptable — and looked at the cameras.

'This is not just about one building or one clause or one company. It is about a system that has been using the law to bury the truth. We are done letting it.'

In the days that followed, more whistleblowers emerged. Labour unions mobilised. A class action by construction workers injured on sites where Clause 14.7 had been deployed began to take shape, led by Maria Taukiri, a scaffolder who had broken her spine on a site where the inspections had been deferred for eleven months.

The system was unravelling.

Elena received a message from Catherine: Judgment Monday. We expect full affirmation.

She stared at the screen, the familiar anxiety and anticipation coursing through her in equal measure. The final word was coming.

But she knew already that the story was not over. This was merely the beginning of a larger fight.

Chapter Twenty-Three

## Judgment Delivered

*Queensland Court of Appeal — Monday morning*

The courtroom was charged with a silence that felt physical. Elena sat beside Liz, Gareth, Marcus, and Catherine Doyle. The gallery was packed. Journalists. Workers. Union representatives. People who had no direct stake in the judgment but had followed its approach the way people follow a storm – not because they can stop it, but because they need to know where it lands.

Justice Elisa Carr entered with the solemnity of someone carrying the weight of her office. In her hand, a folder. Her reasons for judgment.

As she settled into her seat, the silence deepened. The Court Officer's voice broke it: 'This Honourable Court of Appeal is now in session.'

Justice Carr began.

'This appeal arises from a trial concerning the use of Clause 14.7, a contractual provision designed to delay safety inspections in Queensland construction projects. The trial judge found that the clause was deployed with knowledge of its risks and that its concealment contributed to the death of Daniel Ward.'

A ripple of tension through the room.

'The Court affirms the trial judgment in full.'

Elena felt the words land somewhere beneath her ribs.

'The metadata evidence was properly admitted. The whistleblower testimony was credible and corroborated. The damages awarded were proportionate to the harm, the concealment, and the systemic nature of the conduct. The fresh evidence tendered on appeal — the Doyle memo — confirms rather than disturbs the trial judge's findings on intent.'

She turned to Fortis's counsel.

'The appeal is dismissed. Costs will follow the event.'

A wave of emotion swept the plaintiffs' bench. Elena closed her eyes. Beside her, Liz exhaled something that might have been a laugh or might have been a sob. Gareth, across the table, pressed both hands flat on the surface in front of him.

Marcus Hall said nothing. His eyes were full.

Within hours, the headlines ran:

*'Appeal Dismissed: Fortis and Lang Held Liable' — ABC News*

*'Justice for Daniel Ward: Court Affirms Cover-Up' — The Signal*

*'Industry Reckoning: Safety Clause Ruled Unlawful' — The Courier-Mail*

The Premier issued a statement: 'The courts have spoken. Reform must follow.'

Lang & Associates announced a complete leadership restructure. Fortis Constructions confirmed it would not pursue a High Court appeal.

Justice Merrick was placed on indefinite administrative leave pending the Judicial Commission's final report.

In the days following the judgment, Elena was invited to participate in a series of media interviews. She accepted some and declined others, applying the same precision to the choice of her public words as she applied to her legal ones. She was not a symbol. She was a solicitor. She wanted people to understand the difference.

Ward & Associates opened its doors six weeks later: Elena, Liz as partner, and a rotating team of junior lawyers who had heard what the firm stood for and wanted to be part of it.

The work had only just begun.

## Chapter Twenty-Four
## **The Class Action**

The courtroom was larger and more formal than any Elena had stood in before. The gallery was filled with construction workers — many in high-visibility vests, the orange and yellow of them spreading through the rows like a field. They had come from sites across Queensland, from Sydney, from Perth. Some had driven through the night.

Lead plaintiff Maria Taukiri sat at the front, flanked by her legal team. She was forty-one, compact, and carried herself with the quiet authority of someone who has been through something terrible and has decided that the most useful thing to do with it is to stand in a room like this and say so.

The case was Taukiri & Others v Fortis Constructions Pty Ltd. Elena sat behind the legal team as strategic adviser, Liz beside her. Gareth was in the gallery. They had all agreed, without needing to discuss it, that today belonged to the plaintiffs.

Justice Malcolm Reeve took his seat. A hush fell over the courtroom — not the performed quiet of deference, but the genuine silence of a room that understands the weight of what it contains.

Lead counsel Sophie Renshaw rose.

'This case is about harm — physical, financial, and moral. Clause 14.7 was not a mistake. It was a mechanism. A deliberate tool, used across multiple sites over multiple years, to prioritise profit over the lives of the people who built this city. These plaintiffs are here today to ensure that is said, clearly, in a room where it cannot be redacted.'

Maria took the stand later that morning. She spoke for thirty-five minutes. She did not raise her voice. She described the day the scaffolding gave way, the eleven months of deferred inspections that preceded it, the settlement offer she had been given six weeks after leaving hospital — the clause printed in light grey on the eighth page of a document she had been asked to sign quickly.

'I didn't know what it meant,' she said. 'That's the point. That's always the point. They write it so you won't know.'

Kieran Doyle testified again, confirming the deployment of Clause 14.7 across fourteen sites.

Justice Reeve listened to the entire case with the attentiveness of a man who intends his judgment to be, above all else, accurate.

On the final day of argument, Sophie Renshaw addressed the bench: 'Your Honour, we are not asking you to punish Fortis Constructions. We are asking you to describe what they did. The punishment will follow from the description.'

Fortis's counsel, David Kwan, offered a measured defence: the clause was legal, the advice was sought and followed, the plaintiffs were seeking to rewrite contracts through litigation.

The jury retired.

They were out for nine hours.

When the foreperson stood, the courtroom held itself so still that Elena could hear the air conditioning.

'In the matter of Taukiri & Others v Fortis Constructions Pty Ltd, we find in favour of the plaintiffs. We affirm that Clause 14.7 was unlawfully applied and constituted a breach of duty contributing to the injuries and hardships suffered by the plaintiffs.'

The orange and yellow of the gallery rose to its feet.

Elena sat very still for a moment, watching them. The workers who had driven through the night to be in this room. The families behind them. The long, patient weight of people who had been told their suffering was procedurally acceptable, who had decided that it was not.

Justice Reeve delivered his formal judgment two days later: twelve point four milFortis dollars in damages. Clause 14.7 declared unlawful and unenforceable. The matter referred to the Australian Law Reform Commission for a comprehensive review of subcontractor liability clauses.

The Workplace Integrity Amendment Bill passed Parliament the following month: a ban on clauses that delay mandatory inspections, mandatory disclosure of subcontractor terms to regulators, whistleblower protections for all construction workers, a National Safety Clause Registry.

Reform had found its way into law. Not easily, and not without cost. But it was there now, in the language of the statute books, where it could not be quietly settled.

## Chapter Twenty-Five
**Legacy**

The memorial plaque was installed on a Tuesday morning, at the base of the Southbridge construction site entrance, on a section of fence that the workers had agreed to keep clear.

It read:

*In Memory of Daniel Ward*

*Who spoke when others stayed silent.*

Elena stood in front of it for a long time without saying anything. The site behind the fence was active again — rebuilt under new management, new oversight, regular inspections whose completion was now publicly logged in the National Safety Clause Registry. The sound of machinery and voices came over the fence with the ordinary purposefulness of people building things.

Liz stood beside her. Gareth was a few steps back, hands in his pockets, looking at his shoes.

'You changed the law,' Liz said.

'We changed the system,' Elena replied. She meant it. The distinction mattered.

'Do you think it's enough?'

Elena looked at the plaque. At Daniel's name in the bronze. At the words beneath it: Who spoke when others stayed silent.

'It's a start,' she said. 'The law changes faster than the culture that produces it. The culture is the hard part.'

Gareth moved forward and stood beside them. For a while, the three of them were simply three people standing in front of a plaque that had not existed a month ago, in a city that had been changed, in ways large and small and not yet fully legible, by what they had done.

Then Gareth reached into his bag and produced a folder.

He held it out. Elena took it.

Inside: a contract. Mining sector. Western Australia. The clause was on page twelve, buried in the subcontractor indemnity provisions, its language slightly different but its intent unmistakable. Deferred inspection rights. Non-binding safety framework. Liability shifted downstream.

Clause 9.3. Deferred Oversight Protocol.

'How many sites?' Elena asked.

'At least fourteen that I've found so far,' Gareth said. 'Probably more.'

'How long has it been in use?'

'The earliest contract I've seen is 2020. Which means it was probably designed in 2019 or earlier.' He paused. 'After Clause 14.7 started attracting attention. Someone improved the design.'

Elena looked at the folder. Then she looked at the plaque. Then she looked at Liz.

Liz's expression was already set, already calculating, already somewhere three steps ahead of where they were standing.

'Then we're starting again,' Elena said.

'And this time we're faster,' Liz said. 'We know the terrain.'

Gareth nodded once. He looked, Elena thought, lighter than he had looked since the lookout. The guilt was not gone — it would probably never be entirely gone — but it had been put to work. That was something.

She tucked the folder into her satchel beside her notebook, in which Daniel's union card was still pressed against the front cover, a little more worn than it had been two years ago.

Behind the fence, the machinery kept working. The city kept building. The river kept moving.

She had a case to prepare.

## Chapter Twenty-Six
# Echoes

Six months later.

The Ward & Associates offices occupied the eighth floor of a building on Adelaide Street, two blocks from the courthouse. The reception area was modest — Liz had overruled Elena's instinct to spend as little as possible on furnishings, on the grounds that a firm clients trusted needed to look like a firm clients could trust. There were plants. There was natural light. There was a framed print of the Brisbane river at dawn on the wall behind the reception desk, because Elena had chosen it and nobody had argued.

It was, she often thought, a very long way from a document review room on the fourteenth floor of someone else's building.

The Workplace Integrity Amendment Bill had been in force for four months. The National Safety Clause Registry had logged its first five hundred contracts. Three other law firms had voluntarily reviewed their contract libraries and removed provisions that resembled Clause 14.7. Lang & Associates had undergone a leadership restructure and appointed an independent oversight panel; their new managing partner had written Elena a brief, formal letter acknowledging the firm's role in what had happened and committing to reform. She had read it twice and filed it.

The parliamentary inquiry had concluded its hearings. Its final report recommended fifteen legislative changes, all of which the government had agreed, in principle, to implement. Peter Halstead had been referred to the integrity commission. Justice Merrick had retired from the bench, quietly, before the Judicial Commission delivered its findings.

The class action damages had been paid in full.

Maria Taukiri had used part of her share to establish a worker safety education fund. She had asked Elena to be a patron. Elena had said yes.

It was a Thursday. Elena was at her desk by seven-thirty, reviewing submissions for the first Western Australian mining matter, which was scheduled for a directions hearing the following week. Rafiq's forensic analysis of the Clause 9.3 contracts was sitting in a folder at her elbow — thorough, clear, already capable of withstanding the cross-examination it would inevitably face. They were better prepared than they had been for Clause 14.7. They knew the machinery now. They knew the people. They knew the arguments that would be made against them and the arguments they would make in return.

Gareth knocked on the open door at eight. He was carrying two coffees and wearing an expression she had learned, over the past year, to read as cautiously good news.

'The third mine has confirmed. The safety officer is willing to testify.'

'Good,' Elena said. She took the coffee. 'Get me a deposition date.'

He nodded and disappeared back into the corridor.

Liz arrived at eight-fifteen, already talking before she reached Elena's door: 'The Perth journalist wants a background briefing before we file. I think we give it to her — she covered Southbridge fairly and she understands the legal context. Agreed?'

'Agreed.'

'Also,' Liz said, in the slightly different tone that indicated she was about to say something she had been thinking about for longer than she was letting on, 'I spoke to Sophie Renshaw yesterday. There are three agricultural worker groups in the Lockyer Valley who have approached her about a separate matter. She thinks it might be in our wheelhouse.'

Elena looked up from the submissions. 'What kind of matter?'

'Wage theft clauses. Buried in contract translations. Possibly a deliberate mistranslation in one key provision.' A pause. 'The workers are mainly Filipino.'

Elena held Liz's gaze for a moment. The office was quiet around them — the particular quiet of a Thursday morning before the day had properly started, the sound of the city outside coming through the glass at a remove.

'Send Sophie my number,' she said.

Liz nodded. She was already typing.

Elena turned back to the mining submissions. Outside the window, the river moved through the city as it always had — patient, indifferent, carrying the scent of the lush world beyond the office towers. The same river. The same light. The same city building itself upward and outward, its contracts and its clauses and its small, deliberate evasions buried in the fine print of things that were never meant to be read.

But someone was reading them.

She always had been.

*— End of Book One —*

Elena Ward returns in:

***No Verdict for the Dead***

Book Two of the Elena Ward Legal Thriller series